PRACTICAL MODERN
EDUCATIONAL DANCE

To my dear sister,
who unreservedly helped,
inspired and encouraged.

PRACTICAL
MODERN EDUCATIONAL DANCE

with

Suggested Studies

BY
CLAUDETTE COLLINS

MACDONALD & EVANS LTD.
8 JOHN STREET, LONDON W.C.1.
1969

First published October 1969

©

MACDONALD AND EVANS LTD.

1969

S.B.N. 7121 1625 7

Printed in England by The Whitefriars Press Limited, London and Tonbridge

AUTHOR'S PREFACE

THE phase of advocating, persuading or justifying the usefulness of modern dance has long passed, and the art of movement has now taken its rightful place among its sister arts, bringing with it a wealth of material to the service of the development of the creative faculty. Consideration of the brief training periods allocated to the subject, and instant request by student teachers for a simplified dance curriculum, prompted the writing and scheme of this book. After a short introductory chapter, Chapters Two to Four deal respectively with the teaching of Infants, Juniors and Secondary children, while the last chapter offers a number of suggestions which will be helpful to teachers of all three age-groups.

It should be borne in mind that, like all arts, imaginative dance work has no dogmatic formulae, but, movement being one of the most abstract media, it often defies equivalent verbal illustration; for it is intangible, invisible, excepting the body and the limbs which are seen moving, and inaudible, except when in contact with an obstacle, for instance falling, stamping, or clapping. At best it can be illustrated through itself, *i.e.* through movement.

Therefore a fair number of studies have been included in the text. These, however, should not be regarded as strict didactic drill, for they are personal, based on Laban's movement themes, which provide copious material for individual invention, open to anyone studying modern dance. The abundant examples in each topic can be utilised successively in several teaching periods, but, as they are by no means exhaustive, they can be altogether replaced by new ideas.

The music that is suggested for accompaniment consists of short pieces and excerpts selected from a variety of composers whose work appears to concord with the movement qualities. A competent pianist would no doubt discern at a glance the kind of music needed, and thus be able to adapt or improvise her own accompaniment.

Most schools where modern dance is practised are usually well stocked with musical literature, sheet music and records. If an adequate set of percussive instruments is not available, a reasonable collection can be acquired provided that the school is willing to do so.

August 1969   C.C.

CONTENTS

Chapter One

INTRODUCTION

DANCING is an instinctive inclination, an inborn rhythmic urge, involved in man's activities throughout history, wherever he settled as a tribe or a nation. Work and leisure, war and peace, joy, sorrow, fear and hope, birth and death, prayer and thanksgiving, all aspects of life which stirred man's innermost being, were exteriorised through his surging bodily rhythms.

This deep-rooted urge of rhythmic expression is intensely alive in every child. The happy baby on his mother's lap, wriggles, jerks and bounces with obvious delight. The boy let free skips cheerfully away, kicks up one leg, and suddenly takes off in a splendid leap. A group of small girls, often oblivious of time and place, are seen spinning round and round, filling the space with most fascinating gestures. Children enjoy submerging in dance, where they build a world of their own, out and away from the repetitive commonplace of their daily existence.

The teacher can deepen this child's world of fantasy, this inner world, and help children to communicate it through an ordered, coherently articulate language, the language of movement.

The vocabulary of movement is fully provided by Laban's sixteen movement themes. These are set out in two groups of eight, both groups being logically developed. The first comprises elementary working material, the second advanced. The themes of both grades are interdependent, and, since each consists of essential movement components, the order in which they can be taught is optional, provided they follow a progressive plan in accordance with age and ability. All factors in the themes are equally relevant, and should therefore be specifically stressed, in order to direct the children's attention to the effect of the elements, and their relation to one another in an action, a sequence or a dance.

Free working time for exploring, experimenting and inventing should be allowed in the course of a lesson. A well-planned lesson brings joy to both teacher and pupils. Enthusiasm, patience and consideration of the children's potentialities will bring forth gratifying results.

Rudolf Laban

One of the varied epithets attributed to Rudolf Laban during his lifelong work was conferred on him by C. Reissner, the publisher of his autobiography (*Ein Leben fur den Tanz*, 1935), describing him as the "father" of the then new European dance, now the art of movement.

This epithet could equally apply to Laban's fatherly relationship with his co-workers, and students who came to him from different continents of the globe. Though always deeply absorbed in his work, compiling, sifting, analysing and classifying movement material, sorting out the varied aspects of dance history throughout the world, or busily engaged in organising dance groups, shows or large-scale festivals, Laban none the less found time to attend to the cares of those around him, and never withheld a helping hand to those in need, despite his often precarious livelihood.

Chapter Two

INFANTS

THE age in which systematic dancing should begin is often discussed, but, although the six-year-olds are considered eligible, younger children seem to do quite well in the hands of a happily disposed teacher.

Dancing should be based on the child's functional actions, within the scheme of Laban's movement themes. The child uses the whole body in such actions as walking, running, crawling, rolling; both upper and lower body-parts simultaneously (activated by the waist zone) in curling up and falling; both arms for grasping, pulling and pushing; both legs in hopping and kicking when lying down. These simple actions can be applied to developing the child's capability of using its individual limbs, joints and muscles.

Its co-ordination and balance being yet in the initial stage, the child is happiest on the floor where work appropriate to its early concepts can be carried out to its enjoyment. Its distinctively strong and quick movements can be logically transposed into the opposites, *i.e.* the light and slow qualities. And the child's hesitance regarding directions, especially concerning its right and left, can be overcome by verbal indications which tell him, for example, to go to this or the other wall, the corner, the window and so on.

The expression of the child's movements can be developed through mimetic work, movement plays and children's poems relating to the topic being taught (time qualities, dynamics, etc.).

If a poem is used, it should be thoroughly explained, and the actions in each stanza determined. Suggestions should be

3

elicited from the children, and their awkward attempts at interpretation patiently considered.

After context and diction have been clarified and established, the poem can be read as an accompaniment. A well-read poem not only helps rhythmically but also sustains the sequence of the actions. (*See also* Dramatisation, p. 68.)

SETTLING IN

The normal infant, although playful in nature, is overwhelmed by the unfamiliar atmosphere and the new routine at school. Movements in the form of free play will help him to overcome his bewilderment, and soon absorb him in the group, among whom he will enjoy gambolling along, heartily repeating any activity which catches his artless fancy. Yet discretion should be used lest he tires, and brief recuperative moments should therefore be allowed.

Studies

(a) *Meeting, parting:*

(i) Dispersed all round, run and meet in the middle of the room, halt; walk back to place.

(ii) Repeat movement while hopping.

(b) *On the floor:*

(i) Lying, shake limbs; flutter hands, feet.

(ii) Curl up into a ball, stretch; roll like a log.

(iii) Crawl on all fours.

(iv) Sitting, slide anywhere.

(v) Run, sit, rise; repeat actions.

(c) *Movement play.* "Out in the Rain."

1. Under overcast skies, the children are out for a walk, carrying imaginary umbrellas.

2. Sounds of thunder and the chilly raindrops set the children shivering.

3. They fasten their clothes, and open their umbrellas.

4. A "shelter" is sighted and pointed at.

5. All run across puddles, and huddle under "shelter."

STIMULI. Percussion. (*See* Use of Percussion, p. 71.)

TIME QUALITIES

Time is one of the essential components of movement, for all movement takes time during its performance, which can be quick or slow. Quick movements travel a short stretch in space, and terminate abruptly. Slow movements travel relatively longer stretches, and involve continuous muscular exertion. Both qualities promote rhythmic sensitivity.

The two variants can be brought home to the children either by accelerating a series of slow movements or, reversely, by slowing down the preceding quick actions. Although the children prefer quick actions, experience of both qualities brings about a harmonious bodily and mental attitude.

Studies

(*a*) *Slow:*

(*i*) Walk slowly across the floor, then sink slowly.

(*ii*) Lying, curve into crescent shapes: forwards, sideways, and backwards.

(*iii*) In stance, repeat the crescent shapes.

(*b*) *Quick:*

(*i*) Run, halt; clap while turning a full turn; repeat to the other side.

(*ii*) Skip, halt, stamp while turning a full turn; repeat.

(*c*) *Movement play.* "Across the Winding River."

1. Run in the winding path of an imaginary river.

2. Cross carefully over the narrow rickety planks.

3. Run along the prickly path.

4. Find small pebbles and throw them gently into the calm river.

5. Clap hands for joy at the sight of the ripples.

6. Cross back (repeating the crossing actions above).
7. Find a grassy spot and rest.

STIMULI. Percussion.

DYNAMIC QUALITIES

All movement requires a certain amount of force, and is thus either light or strong.

The children's natural tendency for using strong movements should be contrasted with work in the light quality, for both strong and light movements afford new material for exploration and their contrasting effect intensifies the feel, *i.e.* the kinaesthetic sense, of the two qualities.

The importance to the children of watching the inventive results of their companions should not be overlooked, for this increases the observation faculty, and develops aesthetic discrimination.

Studies

(*a*) *Strong, but slow:*
  (*i*) Front leg flexed, push a "heavy object"; lilt back and withdraw arms; repeat *ad libitum*.
  (*ii*) Pull the object back to place; lilt forwards and pull again; repeat.

(*b*) *Strong, but quick:*
  (*i*) Fling a long whip all round the body.
  (*ii*) Punch, kick in all directions.

(*c*) *Light, but quick:*
  (*i*) Flick away the pestering insects.
  (*ii*) Rap on an imaginary pane.
  (*iii*) Sitting, tap the floor with the hands or the toes.

(*d*) *Light, but slow:*
  (*i*) Glide on a slippery surface.
  (*ii*) Rise on toes, and float in the light breeze.

(*e*) *Dancing.* A small group of children dance one of the above movement qualities while the others watch. Change the groups until all have danced.

STIMULI. Percussion.

DIRECTIONS

Directions are the backbone of orientation upon which the shape of movement depends.

In advanced study it is necessary to learn a complex web of orientational directions criss-crossing the space around the body, but at this stage the children should merely become aware of those which are fundamental. These are:

up—down;
forwards—backwards;
right—left.

Most children move exclusively forwards, face leading, which often cuts short the flow of ideas. The awareness of additional directions, together with the possibility of changing the leading body-part, furthers the continuity of the conceived invention. A child seen hesitating, in search of the next move, can be helped by a hint that he change his direction through siding, backing or part-turning through a jump.

Studies

(*a*) *Up–down:*
(*i*) Arms stretched towards ceiling, bounce high and sink.
(*ii*) Walk on toes; sit down and clap.

(*b*) *Forwards–backwards:*
(*i*) Arms forwards, skip forwards; arms backwards, retreat.
(*ii*) Trunk forwards, gallop; step backwards, making wide steps.

(*c*) *Side–side* (right–left):
(*i*) Slip–step sideways; repeat to the other side.
(*ii*) Making wide steps sideways, stamp with the leading foot; stamping with the closing foot, return to place.

(d) *Poem:*

Keep Still

Look, and keep very still,
Still as a tree,
And if you do, you will
Presently see
The doe come down to drink
Leading her fawn
Just as they did, I think,
In the first dawn.

Hark, not a sound, my dear,
Be quiet and hark,
And very soon you'll hear
The vixen bark,
And see her cubs at play
As I believe
They played in starlight grey
On the first eve.

Look, and keep very still.
Hark, not a sound!
The pretty creatures will
Soon be around,
At play and drink, as though
They drank and played
Cub, vixen, fawn and doe,
Ere men were made.

E. FARJEON

This poem can be played by four groups:

1. In the foreground, children dance quietly, freely or in a circle.
2. The "trees" are further back (to the right of group 1):

they are curled up on the floor, then bring out slowly one arm, then the other arm; spread out one finger after the other, like growing leaves; raise the head; grow slowly taller; sway in the gentle breeze.

3. The "pond" are also further back than group 1 (to the left): they each curve their bodies into a half-moon shape and move lightly from side to side, making "water ripples."

4. The "pretty creatures" (hiding behind the "trees") appear, and advance towards the "pond" for a drink.

All the children, except the "pond," express surprise, then follow the "creatures" with love and tenderness.

(*See* Dramatisation, p. 68.)

MUSIC. (The letter preceding each entry shows which study is referred to.)

(*a*) and (*b*) The Knight of the Hobby Horse. Schumann, *Scenes of Childhood*, Op. 15.

(*c*) Quite Happy. *Idem.*

(*d*) Morning Prayer. Tschaikowsky, *Album for the Young*, Op. 39.

SPACE AWARENESS

Space is the vacant expanse surrounding the dancer, his essential requisite, just as is canvas, clay or stone to the artist. Ample space is therefore indispensable.

The dancer, using his body, fills the space with movement patterns varied in size, effort qualities and directions, the material with which he expresses his feelings, thoughts and moods.

Space can be introduced to the children by performing wide and narrow movements, carried from the body into space, and from space towards the body. Outward-flowing movements result in stretching actions; those converging towards the body result in flexing and bending.

To the expert eye, the children's movements appear rough-hewn, but they are spontaneous, natural and sincere. These valuable attributes should be encouraged and fostered. Correcting should therefore be avoided, except when assisting the less able child.

Studies

(a) *Towards the body:*

   (i) Kneeling, hold arms extended; bring arms from different points in space, towards body.

   (ii) In stance, lead arms, a knee, a foot, towards body.

   (iii) Skipping, snatch movements lightly, from all points in space, and bring them in towards body.

(b) *From body into space:*

   (i) Arms near waist, lead them slowly into various directions.

   (ii) In stance, push head upwards; chest forwards; shoulders backwards; hips sideways.

   (iii) Galloping, kick out with free leg.

(c) *Poem:*

The Windmill

Behold, a giant am I!
Aloft here in my tower,
With my granite jaws I devour
The maize, and the wheat, and the rye
And ground them into flour.

I look down over the farms;
In the fields of grain I see
The harvest that is to be,
And fling to the air my arms,
For I know it is all for me.

I hear the sound of flails,
Far off, from the threshing-floors
In barns, with their open doors,
And the wind, the wind in my sails,
Louder and louder roars.

I stand here in my place,
With my foot on the rock below,
And whichever way it may blow
I meet it face to face,
As a brave man meets his foe.

And while we wrestle and strive,
My master, the miller, stands,
And feeds me with his hands;
For he knows who makes him thrive,
Who makes him lord of lands.

On Sundays I take my rest;
Church-going bells begin
Their low, melodious din;
I cross my arms on my breast,
And all is peace within.

LONGFELLOW

This poem is best danced if the class is divided into small groups. The simplicity of style, the familiarity of diction and the almost manifest actions should prove an easy subject for the children's own interpretation; they might even suggest the shape of the group construction, if a good illustration of a windmill is shown. But help for the final touch will no doubt be needed.

The text can be spoken either by a small group of "narrators" placed outside the dancers, or by the leader of each group speaking alternately.

The leader should be picked for his robust build and good voice; as the axis of the construction, he should be placed on a raised surface, roomy enough for his safety, yet allowing for his close contact with those of the group forming his "wings."

Each stanza provides an opportunity for a resting moment during which the narration can be carried out; this of course means that the first stanza will be narrated while the children assemble quietly into their formations.

Often the spoken verse need only be softly prompted by the teacher, but, if speaking talent among the children is not found, the teacher's voice becomes indispensable.

ACCOMPANIMENT

(a) and (b) Percussion.

(c) No. 1 from Seven Rustic Dances. Beethoven, *Complete Dances*, Book II.

Note. The music for (c) can be replaced by suitably adapted percussion.

LEVELS

Levels are the result of an approximate division of space into three horizontal movement strata of high, medium and low planes in relation to the floor:

(a) Lying, sitting, kneeling.

(b) Bending and arching.

(c) Rising, jumping (or leaping).

The levels, together with the directions, provide the dancer with a wide range of situations which affect the movement pattern. For example, a movement established in a certain level will acquire a new aspect when transposed into another, especially when the direction has also been changed.

Levels and directions are vital constituents of architectural shapeliness, particularly important in group constructions.

Studies

(a) *Low:*

   (i) Lying, make slow, light arm and leg movements.

   (ii) Sitting, make small arm movements near body, increasing gradually into space.

(b) *Medium:*

   (i) Kneeling, bend and arch.

   (ii) In stance, twist trunk around waist.

(c) *High:*

   (i) Sitting, rise slowly and walk on toes.

   (ii) Run and jump.

(d) *Exploring.* Dance freely, using levels and directions.

MUSIC

(a) and (b) An Old Dance. Kabalevsky, *Fifteen Children's Pieces.*

(c) A Little Fairy Tale. *Idem.*

(d) First Loss. Schumann, *Album for the Young,* Op. 68.

MUSCULAR CONTROL

Control of the body-parts depends upon spontaneous muscular response to the intended action. Spontaneity can be achieved through aiming at simultaneous reactions of the opposedly situated limbs, *e.g.* the right arm and left leg.

Since this process proves slow and exacting, practice should be brief, but frequently intercalated in already familiar activities.

Studies

(a) *Sitting:*

   (i) Without touching, glide alternate hand along alternate extended arm.

   (ii) Pat opposite alternate thigh.

(b) *In locomotion:*

(i) Galloping, touch the free knee with opposite hand.

(ii) Stepping sideways, slap free foot with opposite hand.

(iii) Skipping, touch the opposite free toe.

(c) *Inventing.* Make a dance of study (b).

MUSIC

(a) Prelude No. 3. Chopin, *Preludes*, Vol. 34.

(b) and (c) The Wild Horseman. Schumann, *Album for the Young*, Op. 68.

MOVEMENT COMPLETION

Children, as well as all beginners, tend to leave off their movements in the midst of an action, a fact clearly manifested by the sudden disappearance of the tensions in the acting muscles.

It is essential that the movement is brought to a definite conclusion by holding it in a momentary state of "stillness," in which, far from resting or relaxing, a relative degree of tension is still exerted. These finer tensions develop muscular sensitivity, the basis of the kinaesthetic sense. Moreover, the conclusion of a movement has the same value as that of a punctuation mark used in a written phrase, a sentence or a paragraph, and is just as important in a dance composition of multiple movement motifs.

Momentary stillness sensation can be roused through statuesque halts, drawn on sensory, emotive or imitative postures.

(a) *Sensory:* looking or listening intently; feeling the breeze on the face, or the raindrops on the extended limbs; fumbling in the dark; etc.

(b) *Emotive:* happiness, sorrow, amazement, fright, humility, pride, etc.

(c) *Imitative:* like a strong, weak or old person; a fairy, an angel, a witch, etc.

In addition, occupational postures, such as chopping wood, watering the flower-bed or hanging up clothes, can be elicited from the children.

Studies

(a) *Pausing during quick movements:*
  (i) Run, skip or gallop; pause suddenly and listen.
  (ii) Spin; pause as if frightened.

(b) *Halting during slow movements:*
  (i) Roll; halt, being surprised.
  (ii) Crawl; sit up suddenly.
  (iii) Row a boat; salute.

(c) *Movement play.* "Abruptly."
  1. Sit or lie motionless, in varied positions.
  2. Rise jerkingly; halt when risen.
  3. Arms extended, trip away; halt.
  4. Bend slowly, halt; arch, redress, halt.
  5. Spin; halt suddenly.
  6. With halts, reach forwards, upwards, to either side, downwards.
  7. Both arms to one side, spin slowly; collapse.

ACCOMPANIMENT. Percussion.

RHYTHMIC STRESS

Movements are stressed through dynamic intensity, speed, directions and levels, just as speech is modulated through pace, pitch, tone and volume, which give light and shade to the rhythmic aspect by setting the stronger points in bold relief.

An accent in a movement may occur at the beginning, in the middle or at the end. Movement sequences may contain several accents of different values, but the children should first experience the single types until they are well grasped.

Studies

   (*a*) *Accent at the beginning:*

      (*i*) Jump, run; decrease to walking pace.

      (*ii*) Shake body, gradually decreasing; lie slowly down.

   (*b*) *Accent at the end:*

      (*i*) Walk, increasing pace; jump.

      (*ii*) Curl up, open slowly while rising; spin, increasing speed; halt suddenly.

   (*c*) *Accent in the middle:*

      (*i*) Walk, increasing to running pace; jump, run, decreasing to slow walking.

      (*ii*) Open slowly one arm, then the other; add a leg; close up quickly; sink slowly.

   (*d*) *Exploring.* Make phrases of single accents.

STIMULI. Percussion.

FLOOR PATTERNS

Floor patterns eliminate the haphazard wandering, draw the mover into definite paths, and set movement phrases into a neatly designed plan.

Through the simple pattern of a rectangle, a zigzag or a triangle, the child will realise that while dancing his feet can trace invisible lines, and that these lines can be conceived in advance.

Designs of complicated orientation, such as spirals or the figure "8," should be reserved for later studies, when the sense of orientation has been strengthened.

Studies

   (*a*) *Rectangles:*

      (*i*) Walk parallel to the walls, spinning at each corner.

      (*ii*) Making a smaller rectangle, run, kneeling at each corner.

(b) *Triangles:*

  (i) Skip along two adjacent walls; walk, clapping hands, along the diagonal which cuts through the rectangle.

  (ii) Facing the wall which leads to the second triangle, slide sideways on the diagonal; stamp at the corner, and complete the remaining parts of the pattern.

(c) *Zigzags:*

  (i) Walking in single file, jump at each point.

  (ii) Tripping, cut out the points.

(d) *Exploring.* Individually, find a space and dance in a definite floor pattern, remembering directions and levels.

MUSIC

  (a) A Northern Song. Schumann, *Album for the Young.*

  (b) and (c) Rustic Song. *Idem.*

  (d) Song of the Reapers. *Idem.*

SPACE PATTERNS

Space patterns are the visible movement forms; these have complex characteristics, the grasp of which is at this stage beyond the children's capacity. The outer forms, however, can be introduced to the children through simple drawings in space, similar to those of the floor patterns: straight lines, zigzags, triangles, squares, curves and circles. The patterns can be narrow, near the body or extend to their fullest into space.

The idea of making shapes in space can be instilled through the use of the children's normal drawing tool, their hands. Once awareness of the possibilities has been awakened, other body-parts, *e.g.* elbows and knees, can be used for drawing smaller patterns, while the extremities of the limbs will be useful for constructing those of wider forms. One should also experiment with steps in order to see whether they harmonise with the movements of the upper body-parts.

Obviously, the smaller the movements, the shorter will be

their time duration. Walking, sliding and, to some extent, hopping are easily adaptable to slower movements, while the time values of running, skipping and tripping will serve the smaller space patterns.

When space patterns are practised, they can be combined with the floor patterns, and dynamics, directions, levels, etc., should not be neglected.

Studies

(a) *Straight lines:*

(i) Sitting, draw single lines, in front of, at either side of and behind the body.

(ii) With alternate hands, draw zigzags around the waist.

(iii) Kneeling, draw a triangle with both hands, above head, behind the shoulders and at either side.

(b) *Curves:*

(i) In stance, leading downwards, make half-circles, in front of, at either side of and below waist; repeat, leading upwards.

(ii) With both arms, draw upright circles in all directions; repeat, making horizontal circles.

(iii) Draw circles and half circles with the free leg.

(c) *Combined space and floor patterns:*

(i) Tripping, make zigzag space and floor patterns.

(ii) Skipping, make triangular space and floor patterns.

(iii) Make wavy curves, up and down, while tripping in a wide circle.

(d) *Exploring.* Make wide and narrow space and floor patterns.

MUSIC

(a) Nos. 1, 2 and 3 from Six Ecossaises. Beethoven, *Complete Dances*, Book II.

(b) Allemande. *Idem.*

(c) No. 5 from Twelve Contre-Dances. *Idem.*

(d) No. 4 from Six Minuets. *Complete Dances*, Book I.

PHRASING

It is too early to discuss the composition of the actual phrasing based on effort actions. But, having become aware of the essence of rhythmic stress and movement completion, the children should be able to make short phrases and sequences derived from the work done hitherto.

A movement word consists of a single action in three parts:

(a) Preparation.

(b) Execution.

(c) Termination.

The action of a jump, for example, will be clearly pronounced by the following:

(a) A few steps increased in pace.

(b) The actual jump.

(c) The landing.

Several movement words, ensuing logically from the initial action, constitute a phrase, expressing purpose and meaning. For example, a jump followed by a spin, and completed by sinking to the floor, will convey a totally different idea from that very same jump if completed by a sprawl and a slow rise.

A movement sequence comprises several phrases, comparable to a full statement of the spoken word.

Studies

(a) *Phrases:*

    (i) Lying, rise slowly; open arms while running; halt, closing arms as if hugging someone, or something.

    (ii) Crouching, begin spinning slowly upwards; gradually increasing speed to running, jump.

    (iii) Run; decrease to walking; kneel; lie down.

(*b*) *Sequences:*

   (*i*) Punch with arms and legs; stamp, decreasing force; sink slowly, roll, sprawl.

   (*ii*) Rise quickly, run, halt; bend slowly to all directions, as if looking for something lost; find it, pick it up lightly, walk away.

   (*iii*) Walk, halt, clap furiously; open arms while running, pause with arms akimbo; sink slowly and curl head to knees.

STIMULI. Percussion throughout.

DANCING WITH A PARTNER

Work with a partner terminates the period of mingling individually with the mass, and brings the children into direct contact with one another. Not only does this fulfil the child's growing desire to share his activities with others, but it also develops his faculty of observation, strengthens his memory and engenders adaptation, co-operation and reciprocity. Thus the process of adjustment to circumstances and people takes place, leading to sound social relationships.

Partners can dance in the following three ways:

   (*a*) *Simultaneously:* meeting, parting and surrounding.

   (*b*) *Responding:* a form of question and answer.

   (*c*) *Imitating:* reproducing an exact copy of the partner's movements.

Studies

   (*a*) *Simultaneously:*

   (*i*) Skipping, part, kneel, rise, turn round, meet; together, make floor patterns.

   (*ii*) Dance round your partner while he dances round himself; change over.

(*b*) *Responding:*

   (*i*) Watch partner, and answer with suitable movements.

   (*ii*) Dance to the sounds of percussion played by your partner; play a different instrument when your turn comes.

(*c*) *Imitating:*

   (*i*) Watch carefully the strong movements of your partner and copy them; make quick movements when your turn comes.

   (*ii*) Make a floor pattern for your partner to copy.

   (*iii*) Make space patterns within a floor pattern.

   (*iv*) Copy your partner's curving space pattern.

STIMULI

   (*a*) No. 1. Schumann, *Scenes of Childhood*, Op. 15.

   (*b*) (*i*) No. 2 *Idem.*

   (*b*) (*ii*) and (*c*) Percussion.

Chapter Three

JUNIORS

JUNIORS can be expected to start dancing with greater confidence and ability than the infant beginner. Some juniors will have had school preparation. Others will have acquired the natural bodily skills of walking, running, skipping, jumping, etc., as dictated by the vital daily pursuits. Yet both categories will need developing a clear expression of their cumulative experiences and deepening sensitivity.

The eight basic themes, with their extensive range of invaluable material, are suitably applicable to beginners of all ages, including adults. Some of the more advanced themes can be used with the older or more able children, since both the elementary and advanced themes are based on the same fundamental principles. The movement terminology, as specified by Laban, should now be used in order to enrich the children's general vocabulary.

The studies in the text should as far as possible be replaced by the children's own experiments after a lesson has been set in motion, but they can be utilised if the class's grasping of the subject appears all too vague.

Free time for individual or group work during the lesson, in the form of a task, will help the children in assimilating the gist of the subject, and enable the teacher to assess the children's comprehension. A task therefore needs no accompaniment nor any stimuli, except when requested by the children who feel the need of some extraneous aid in expressing their ideas.

BODY ZONES

The waist divides the body in two parts: the upper zone, head, arms and trunk; and the lower zone, the legs from hip to toe. Accordingly, each zone moves in its particular area, the space zone.

The upper body zone, being more manipulative, can use both space zones with relative ease through bending and arching. But the legs, excepting the knees, can hardly penetrate the upper space zone unless acrobatically trained. The main role of the legs is to support the body in stance and locomotion.

The conception of the zones can be conveyed to the children through actions first performed by the upper body zone and then by the lower zone – e.g. arm movements above head and around trunk, twisting the trunk around the waist – and, finally, by contrasting these with leg actions reaching out into the upper zone. All these actions are best performed while in stance, with legs parted, so as to secure a firm position.

Once the idea of the zones has been grasped, it should be experienced also in locomotion.

Studies

(a) *Upper zone:*

  (i) In stance, swing arms from side to side, backwards and forwards, above head, deep below waist.

  (ii) Twist round waist while bending, swinging both arms in the same direction as the trunk; repeat to the other side.

(b) *Lower zone:*

  (i) Raise alternate legs slowly, and as high as possible.

  (ii) Stretch alternate legs forwards; backwards; across the body.

  (iii) Try touching the back with alternate feet.

(c) *In locomotion:*

  (i) Step – hop, swinging both arms backwards and for- wards.

  (ii) Skipping, raise free knee close to chest.

(*d*) *Task.* With a partner, make a sequence of study (*c*), using floor patterns.

MUSIC

(*a*) No. 10. Schubert, *Dances*, Book I.

(*b*) No. 11. *Idem.*

(*c*) and (*d*) Hunting Song. Schumann, *Album for the Young.*

GESTURES

A gesture is a wide or narrow movement performed by the limbs, or their parts, when free from supporting the main body weight.

Hands and fingers are most mobile, and can be very expressive. Arm gestures, wide in their nature, can be further extended by bending, or twisting in the waist; by jumps or turns; or by one continuous movement carried from point to point in space, while travelling. Leg gestures transform the ordinary, basic steps into imaginative shapes, harmonising with the arm gestures. Foot gestures are usually small.

Studies

(*a*) *Arm and hand gestures:*

   (*i*) Sitting, make small finger and hand gestures.

   (*ii*) Kneeling, make wide arm gestures around the body.

(*b*) *Leg gestures:*

   (*i*) In stance, make small foot gesture round the supporting leg.

   (*ii*) Travelling, make wide leg gestures.

(*c*) *Arm and leg gestures:*

   (*i*) Tripping, in a zigzag floor path, make wide arm gestures.

   (*ii*) Make small arm gestures while turning.

   (*iii*) Running, jump, making leg gestures.

(*d*) *Task.* Combine arm and leg gestures.

MUSIC

(a) and (b) Quite Happy. Schumann, *Scenes of Childhood*.

(c) An Important Event. *Idem*.

(d) A Sad Story. Kabalevsky, *Fifteen Children's Pieces*.

WEIGHT TRANSFERENCE

The simplest transference of the body weight occurs when the legs are used with the intention of covering a certain distance. But the dancer often transfers his weight onto a part of his body when in a stationary posture, using directions and levels while gesticulating with his free limbs.

When covering distances, however, the dancer cannot avoid using the ordinary steps of walking, running, skipping, jumping, leaping, etc. Yet, knowing the principles of movement, he is able to elaborate the common steps, giving them value and meaning, according to his own conceptions, thus presenting an original product of his imagination.

Studies

(a) *On the floor:*

(i) Supported on the shoulder-blades and the arms, gesticulate with the legs in various directions.

(ii) Sitting, gesticulate with arms and legs.

(iii) Kneeling, gesticulate with alternate arms; with both arms.

(b) *In locomotion:*

(i) Walking, make wide gestures with the free leg.

(ii) Jump, raising both knees to chest; repeat with alternate knees.

(iii) Keeping free leg across body-front, turn while hopping; repeat to the other side.

(c) *Task*. Make a slow dance, starting on the floor, followed by wide gestures of arms and legs while travelling.

MUSIC

(a) No. 1. Two Country Dances. Beethoven, *Master Series for the Young.*

(b) No. 2. *Idem.*

(c) Landler No. 10. Schubert, *Dances*, Book II.

GATHERING – SCATTERING

Gathering–scattering is a succession of swinging gestures expressing the actions of bringing the movement in towards the body, and sending it out from the body into space, which produces a marked sensation of tension and relaxation. The movements are particularly apparent in the upper body zone with a strikingly evident preparation of the arms.

The dynamic stress of the downward course is strongly felt with the effect of gripping and repulsing, resulting in tensions and counter-tensions. But while this develops muscular flexibility it causes accumulative exertion, which requires careful practising.

Natural gathering actions are led by the palms, while scattering actions are led by the back of the hand. Reversing these leading parts restrains the swinging character of the movement. Movements of the legs, rotating in the hips, can be led by the instep, or by the sole of the foot.

Although they do so to a lesser degree, most other body-parts can gather and scatter, and countless movement combinations can be evolved from these swinging actions. For example: in stance, both arms gathering while bending, and scattering while stretching in the up–down direction; both arms swinging while bending followed by immediate stretching in the side–side direction; both arms and the free leg in stance or locomotion; reversing the leading parts when gathering; and so on.

It should be observed that gathering–scattering is an inseparable action, because repeated gathering, for instance, involves scattering, and vice-versa. But either part of this action can be stressed through time qualities and dynamics, the two factors of which the children are no doubt already aware.

(See also R. Laban, *The Mastery of Movement*, p. 87.)

Studies

(a) *Stress on gathering:*
 (i) In stance, gather strongly with alternate arms, scatter lightly.
 (ii) Accented gathering of shoulders, elbows, hips, knees.
 (iii) Gather lightly with both arms and free leg.

(b) *Stress on scattering:*
 (i) In stance, scatter with both arms into various directions; gather with small movements.
 (ii) Scatter slowly alternate arms, gathering quickly, immediately followed by gathering quickly the opposite leg, scattering it slowly.

(c) *Gathering–scattering:*
 (i) Gather while bending; scatter while arching.
 (ii) Skipping, gather–scatter with opposite limbs. (Arms remain still while stepping onto the free leg.)

(d) *Reversed hand-parts leading:*
 (i) Using wide, slow gestures, gather with back of hands, scatter with palms.
 (ii) Gather–scatter, using palms only; back of hands only.

(e) *Task.* With a partner, make a sequence of gathering–scattering.

MUSIC

(a) and (b) No. 15. Fovargue, *Tunes for Movement Classes.*

(c) No. 22. *Idem.*

(d) No. 28. *Idem.*

(e) No. 29. *Idem.*

BALANCE

The spine divides the body into two symmetric parts, situated on the right and on the left. Using one-sided, *i.e.* asymmetric, body-parts while in motion throws the body weight out of balance.

A steady balance entails the simultaneous extension of several symmetrically positioned limbs, proceeding in different directions, in order to equalise the weight of the body. A typical example of distributed weight is the universal walking action in which one arm and the opposite leg are extended forwards, and the other arm backwards.

Regaining firm balance out of strong mobility is particularly exacting, requiring perseverant practice. But the juniors, having acquired the initial skills of walking, running, skipping, etc., should be able to concentrate on studying balance.

While one should practise sparingly, balance should often be included in other movement topics.

Studies

(*a*) *Travelling:*
   (*i*) Walking, mark well the swinging arms.
   (*ii*) Running, halt suddenly on one foot.
   (*iii*) Skipping, halt and arch.

(*b*) *In stance:*
   (*i*) Lean forwards and balance on tip-toes; repeat, balancing on one foot.
   (*ii*) Keeping free leg in front, hop turning a full turn.
   (*iii*) Supported on one leg, balance horizontally forwards; try arching.

(*c*) *Regaining balance:*
   (*i*) Walking, halt suddenly, raising free leg forwards; repeat, raising backwards; then again, raising sideways.
   (*ii*) Running, jump, landing on one foot, then halt; repeat, rising on tip-toe.

(*d*) *Task.* Make a dance of balancing studies.

ACCOMPANIMENT

(*a*) The Stranger. Schumann, *Album for the Young.*

(*b*) and (*c*) The Entreating Child. Schumann, *Scenes of Childhood.*

(*d*) Percussion.

Note. The task should first be worked out by the children according to their choice of study, after which the appropriate instrument can be used either by themselves or by the teacher.

CO-ORDINATION

Co-ordination and balance are inter-related, for co-ordination entails good balance in addition to instantaneous and concerted response to the symmetrically positioned body-parts, which results in harmonious relation between thought and action.

Concordant response can be furthered by simultaneously moving the symmetrically situated limbs into the same or into different directions, *e.g.* one arm and the opposite leg conjointly moving into different directions while the mover progresses forwards, or, alternately, follows one of the leading limbs.

Studying co-ordination demands full mental concentration, and should therefore be first practised in stance, but, since prolonged standing becomes rather tedious, locomotion should be introduced as soon as some degree of co-ordination is apparent.

Studies

(*a*) *In stance:*

(*i*) Swing simultaneously one arm forwards, the other backwards.

    (*ii*) Bend and stretch both arms and alternate legs.

    (*iii*) Stretch one arm forwards, the other sideways with the free leg backwards.

(*b*) *In locomotion:*

    (*i*) Skipping, swing both arms into the direction of the supporting leg.

    (*ii*) Galloping, swing one arm upwards, the other sideways.

    (*iii*) Hopping, swing one arm forwards–up, the other touching the free knee.

(*c*) *Task*. Make a threesome dance, using study (*b*).

MUSIC

    (*a*) Popular Air. Schumann, *Album for the Young*.

    (*b*) and (*c*) The Wild Horse. *Idem*.

RHYTHMIC STRUCTURE

The form and meaning of movement is expressed by its rhythmic structure, composed of time duration, dynamic stress and the rate, or "tempo," at which movement motifs follow one another.

There are two kinds of rhythm:

    (*a*) The *metric* rhythm, consisting of one or several simple movements repeated in succession, assigned mainly to the lower body zone – the legs – as seen in stamping, skipping, galloping, and in the familiar footwork of folk dancing.

    (*b*) The *free* rhythm, composed of varied time duration and unequal stresses, occurring at different intervals within a movement phrase or sequence, and assigned to the upper body zone, particularly to the arms.

That the rhythmic capacity of the lower zone is limited, as compared with the freedom of the upper zone, is due to the fact that the legs are burdened with the role of carrying the weight of the body, whereas the upper zone, being supported by the legs, is able to tip, sway, bend or arch. And the arms, rotating in the shoulders, have remarkable freedom, able to trace most complicated patterns. Hence the dancer's ability to perform simultaneously the two kinds of rhythm: the legs supplying the metric quality, while the upper zone is moving in free "tuneful" rhythmic sequences, just as a tuneful waltz, for example, is accented by the metric chords.

Time duration and dynamic stress can be explained to the children through their familiarity with time qualities and the dynamics of light and strong movements. Tempo can be conveyed by a quick succession of simple movements being repeated in slow consecutive order, or by a slow succession of movements, repeated quickly.

Studies

(a) *Metric rhythm:*

 (i) Stepping sideways, stamp with leading leg; repeat to the other side, stamping with the closing leg; repeat both movements while jumping onto the leading leg.

 (ii) Spring twice on each foot, in any direction.

 (iii) In stance, spring from side to side in succession; repeat, travelling forwards; backwards.

(b) *Free rhythm:*

 (i) Make arm gestures, stressed by hand flicks.

 (ii) Tripping, swing arms slowly from side to side.

 (iii) Walking, move arms in curved patterns.

(c) *Tempo:*

 (i) Walk slowly in zigzag floor patterns, while swinging slowly alternate arms.

 (ii) Repeat study (i), in quick succession.

(d) *Task.* Make a dance of free rhythms.

ACCOMPANIMENT. Percussion throughout.

PATH PATTERNS

The classical circle and its compound forms present a number of turnings, divergences, convergences and orientational complications in relation to the leading body-parts. These require clarification.

The circle can be followed: clockwise, anti-clockwise, facing the direction, backing and siding; and in a similar way towards and away from circle centre.

Clear perception of the spiral can be obtained by forming a wide circle, coiling gradually in towards the centre, and uncoiling when returning to the starting point.

Orientation in the path of the figure "8" often causes concern, especially where two groups are involved. As used in English country dancing this pattern is somewhat elongated, and is mostly danced by three or four people, but in group dancing the shape is invariably transformed into two adjacent circles.

The size of the groups involved is immaterial, but the number of members in one group should be equal to that in the other.

Let us say that two groups, A and B, form two adjacent circles. The children in each group are placed one behind the other; the A group have their right side towards centre, B their left side. All start travelling simultaneously, but before starting it should be made clear whether the children in A are to cross in front or behind those in B. When interchanging of circles begins, the sides of right and left presented to circle centre will reverse; e.g. as soon as A have entered circle B, they will have their left side towards centre. Once travelling orientation has been settled, a full dance can be developed in this path pattern.

Movements may vary from the simplest to the most advanced, depending upon age and ability. Children are fascinated by the path alone, and enjoy discovering the ease in which disentanglement can be accomplished even if it means much walking or skipping. However, hard practising should be avoided.

Studies

(a) *Circle:*

    (i) Individually, step out a circle; retreat, with back leading, to starting point; turn half turn, and with face leading retrace the circle.

    (ii) Slip–step sideways towards centre; leading with the other side, return to place.

(b) *Spiral.* In single file, walk, making a wide circle; now coil in towards centre; turn and retrace the path; repeat with varied steps.

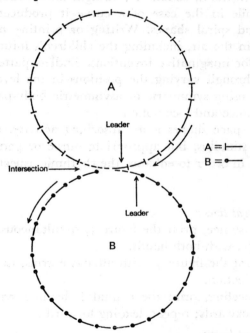

Fig. 1. Figure "8" for two groups.

(c) *Figure* "8." Make two adjacent circles A and B, with the children placed one behind the other. Group A have their right side towards the centre, B their left side.

A continuous path through both circles is now established
at the intersecting point, with the leader of each group
facing the path of the other circle. Start walking simultaneously, and continue walking until everyone has
returned to his place in his original circle. (*See* Fig. 1.)

SPACE SHAPES

Movements assume definite forms of lines and curves in
space; these can be consciously designed through directional
changes.

Change in the direction of a straight line produces angular
shapes, while in the case of a curve it produces undulate,
circular and spiral shapes. Writing or printing numerals or
alphabets in the air, including the children's initials, offers a
vast field for imaginative inventions. Endless patterns can be
invented through varying the positions in the levels and the
directions, using symmetric or asymmetric body-parts of both
zones in stance and locomotion.

Making space shapes is an absorbing activity, needing no
particular stimulus, but appropriate music or percussion can
be applied in order to enhance the rhythmic aspects.

Studies

(*a*) *Straight lines:*
   (*i*) In stance, print the figure 1, simultaneously at either
        side, with both hands.
   (*ii*) Print the figure 4, with alternate arms, in mirror-like
        reflection.
   (*iii*) Kneeling, print the capital I, leading symmetrically
        backwards; repeat, leading forwards.
(*b*) *Curved lines:*
   (*i*) Walking sideways, print the capital C with the leading
        leg.
   (*ii*) Make the floor and space pattern of the capital S.
   (*iii*) Turning, write the figure 8.

(c) *Compound shapes:*
  (i) Print the capital R, led from a jump, down to the floor.
  (ii) Reverse the capital B, back to front.
  (iii) Lying on the floor, print with your legs the capital D lying on its back.
(d) *Task.* In any position, print or write any letters or numerals.

MUSIC

  (a) No. 3. Bach, *Short Preludes and Fugues.*
  (b) No. 5. *Idem.*
  (c) Theme, and Variation I. Beethoven, *Master Series for the Young.*
  (d) Individual work.

WEIGHT

Weight is one of the essential factors of movement; it is related to muscular energy and the force of gravity and affects the quality of movement and the mover's attitude.

The amount of energy, or the effort, employed by the mover qualifies the movement; thus it can be strong and heavy — termed "firm" — or light — termed "fine touch."

The force of gravity creates the mover's attitude, for a firm movement has a downward tendency; when the mover follows this natural trend he indulges in weight. However, if he leads his firm movement upwards, he has to fight against weight.

A similar attitude is created in performing a fine touch movement which tends upwards, effecting an attitude of indulging in lightness. However, when the mover guides his fine touch downwards, he fights against lightness.

The centre of gravity, *i.e.* the point at which weight is equally distributed in both body zones, is located in the region of the pelvic girdle. Lightness, or "levity," is located in the region of the breastbone.

Movements are conveyed through effort actions. The familiar firm actions of pushing, pulling, throwing, kicking, and all similar actions, comprise elements of:

pressing, wringing, thrusting, slashing.

Fine touch actions, such as smoothing, tapping, jerking or similar light actions, comprise elements of:

gliding, floating, flicking, dabbing.

The firm actions of pressing and thrusting and the fine touch actions of gliding and dabbing have straight space patterns. The two remaining firm actions — wringing and slashing — and the two remaining fine touch actions — floating and flicking — have curving space patterns.

Most effort actions are usually carried out in front of the body, and are intensely felt in the upper body zone, particularly in the arms, but the varied finer shades of movement are experienced when the actions are performed around the body while facing forwards.

The actions can be combined into movement phrases, or sequences, but they should first be practised independently.

Studies

(*a*) *Firm actions:*

(*i*) In stance, press both arms forwards; press alternate arms sideways across chest, then backwards, over the opposite shoulder.

(*ii*) In stance, wring hands, arms, upper body zone, the whole body.

(*iii*) Walking, thrust free leg in varied directions.

(*iv*) Running, slash across front with alternate arm; slash both arms backwards, then sideways.

(*b*) *Fine touch actions:*

   (*i*) Walking, flick hands, elbows, free knee, free foot.

   (*ii*) Extend both arms forwards, and float on tip-toes either in varied directions or making floor patterns.

   (*iii*) Walking backwards, dab with shoulders, hips, free knee.

   (*iv*) Lying, flick with alternate hand upwards; raise knees, and flick with alternate foot, then with both feet.

(*c*) *Task.* Respond to a partner with any suitable action.

STIMULI. Suitably applied percussive instruments.

WEIGHT AND TIME

Effort elements being interwoven, both firm and fine touch movements can be slow — termed "sustained" – or quick — termed "sudden." Sustained actions, denoting leisure or purpose, express indulgence in time. Sudden actions, denoting urgency or excitement, imply fighting against time.

The children should first explore each effort separately, using upper and lower body zones, levels and directions. Floor and space patterns should be added after the efforts have been fully experienced.

Studies

(*a*) *Firm sustained:*

   (*i*) Kneeling, press alternate arms in opposite directions.

   (*ii*) Walking sideways, wring hips.

(*b*) *Firm sudden:*

   (*i*) Jumping, thrust arms, then legs.

   (*ii*) Galloping, slash in various directions.

(*c*) *Fine touch sustained:*

   (*i*) Floating, make undulate space shapes.

   (*ii*) Gliding, skate smoothly in straight floor patterns.

(*d*) *Fine touch sudden:*

  (*i*) Running, flick with alternate hands, upwards, down-
    wards and over the opposite shoulder.

  (*ii*) Walking, flick both hands and free foot.

(*e*) *Task.* In small groups dance simultaneously or respond
  with effort actions.

ACCOMPANIMENT

  (*a*) No. 4. Chopin, *Prelude for the Piano*, Vol. 35.

  (*b*) No. 5. *Idem.*

  (*c*) No. 7. *Idem.*

  (*d*) No. 3. *Idem.*

  (*e*) Percussion.

MOVEMENT CHARACTERISTICS

A movement flowing in curved, deviating paths in space,
while changing direction and level, results in a three-dimensional form, is "flexible" in character, and involves indulging
in space.

Movements flowing unswervingly from point to point in
space are "direct" and imply fighting against space.

Wringing, slashing, floating, flicking, and all actions flowing
in twisted paths, are flexible.

Pressing, thrusting, gliding, dabbing, and all their derivatives, are direct.

Stressing these characteristics through already familiar
actions will help one to grasp the two contrasting movement
aspects.

Studies

  (*a*) *Flexible:*

    (*i*) Float, writing the letter S.

    (*ii*) Wring, making spirals in space.

(*iii*) Slash, writing the letter C; repeat, inverting the letter back to front.

(*iv*) Flick, drawing the figure 8.

(*b*) *Direct:*

   (*i*) Press, drawing triangles in space.

   (*ii*) Thrust, drawing radii flowing from body-centre into space.

   (*iii*) Glide in square floor paths.

(*c*) *Task.* Make a dance of direct and flexible movements.

MUSIC

(*a*) Nautilus. MacDowell, *Sea Pieces.*

(*b*) Song. *Idem.*

(*c*) Alone at Sunset. Carroll, *Sea Idylls.*

MOVEMENT FLOW

Laban states:

(*a*) "In an action in which it is difficult to stop a movement suddenly, the flow is *free* or *fluent.*"

(*b*) "In an action capable of being stopped or held without difficulty at any moment during the movement, the flow is *bound.*"

Thus the attitude to free flow is one of yielding to it, indulging in the sensation of moving freely and continuously. The action of initiating a movement sets the flow of that movement, and resisting the force of the established flow means, then, fighting against it, or, alternatively, stopping it at any moment.

Flow is self-revealing, and is easily perceived through experience; for example, slashing is obviously a movement of free flow because a slashing action cannot be stopped before it has run its full course, whereas pressing, on the other hand, can be held at any moment.

Bound flow actions are: pressing, wringing, gliding. Those of free flow are: slashing, flicking, dabbing. Thrusting and floating, however, can be performed either in bound or in free flow.

The sensation of flow can be experienced by trying to stop suddenly in a free-flowing action. Compare the result with what happens in a bound action, in which movement can be easily stopped.

Studies

(*a*) *Free flow:*

    (*i*) In stance, slash with right leg away to the right; left leg to the left.

    (*ii*) Extend right arm high above left shoulder, and slash downwards to the right; repeat with left arm; repeat while jumping.

    (*iii*) In stance, open both arms and dab downwards until both hands meet; return to starting point; repeat while walking in varied directions.

    (*iv*) Step–close sideways and flick simultaneously with one arm downwards, the other upwards on every second step.

(*b*) *Bound flow:*

    (*i*) Walking, press alternate arms away from body, then towards body; press free knee towards chest, then sideways across hips.

    (*ii*) In stance, wring both arms to the left while tipping to the right; repeat to the other side.

    (*iii*) Walking, glide free foot across floor before transferring weight.

    (*iv*) Progressing forwards, press chest gradually forwards with intervening stops; retreating, repeat movement while pressing upper body zone.

(*c*) *Mixed possibility:*

  (*i*) Running, thrust alternate arm backwards; repeat with
  stops.

  (*ii*) Jumping, thrust one leg across body; repeat, thrusting
  away from body.

  (*iii*) Float in zigzag floor pattern; repeat with stops.

ACCOMPANIMENT. Suitably applied percussive instruments.

Chapter Four

SECONDARY CHILDREN

SECONDARY schools present some problems to the newly arrived teacher. A relatively well-established dance tradition might need sorting out, adapting and furthering, and special lines of approach to the varied abilities in the graded streams will have to be conceived.

The first-year groups, especially, will require tactful handling, for they are, as yet, a mixed gathering, coming from many, and varied, schools, who will have been taught dance by different individuals all of whom might well have applied their own personal knowledge and bias. Moreover, the young new entrant, moved by the fact of having reached the stage of secondary tuition, is filled with anticipation, expecting new interests, new information and activities. Therefore, the eventuality of a pupil remarking, resentfully, that this or that has been taught in his or her earlier school should be forstalled by discovering, at the very beginning, the standard of dance in each class.

A lesson with ample scope for deviating from the difficult to the ligher aspects of dance might prove helpful with the more sophisticated groups, whereas the younger pupils can be tested by setting them a task, in small groups, which will soon reveal the general standard and the individual limitations.

THE EIGHT BASIC EFFORT ACTIONS

Dance-making begins when the "feel" of the effort actions has been thoroughly experienced, and when clear identification of their components has been secured.

From his analyses, Laban deduced two principles:

(*a*) That all movement actions, whether occupational or artistic, are based on eight fundamental units or "effort actions."

(*b*) That each of these eight actions contains three of the six components, or factors, pertaining to:

    weight (firm, fine touch);
    time (sudden, sustained);
    space (direct, flexible).

Accordingly, these actions fall into three specific categories by differing in one, two or three factors:

(*a*) Those differing in one factor, but identical in the remaining two, are "primarily akin actions."

(*b*) Those differing in two factors are "secondarily akin actions."

(*c*) Those differing in all three factors are "contrasting actions."

These actions are basic, because they are the constituents of any single movement, sequence or complex dance, comparable to the notes which constitute a musical phrase, passage or entire composition.

The primarily and secondarily akin actions form coherent sequences through direct and gradual transitions respectively. The contrasting actions are used in their intrinsic forms, but transitions, though elaborate, are also possible.

Transitions are operated by increasing or decreasing the power of the differing factors, resulting in a coherent, smoothly flowing sequence. For example, if the differing factor is weight, the firm action will be joined to that of fine touch, either by decreasing the force of the former, or by increasing that of the latter.

1. Primarily akin actions

Transmutation is the operation of changes of the elemental factors affecting the sequence of an effort action. In the case of primarily akin actions this is achieved by immediate intensification or diminution of the differing weight, time or space:

(*a*) *Differing in weight* (akin through space and time): wring–float, slash–flick, thrust–dab, press–glide.

(*b*) *Differing in time* (akin through weight and space): wring–slash, press–thrust, glide–dab, float–flick.

(*c*) *Differing in space* (akin through weight and time): wring–press, slash–thrust, float–glide, flick–dab.

Studies

(*a*) *Transmuting weight:*

   (*i*) Wring–float: float, making undulate patterns of floor and space; increase dynamics to wringing arms, trunk, whole body.

   (*ii*) Slash–flick: travelling, slash, decreasing to flicking.

(*b*) *Transmuting time:*

   (*i*) Wring–slash: in stance, wring hips, shoulders; increasing speed, run, slash in various directions.

   (*ii*) Glide–dab: dab with alternate knee; decreasing speed, glide in zigzag patterns.

(*c*) *Transmuting space:*

   (*i*) Wring–press: wring whole body, gradually straightening; press while travelling.

   (*ii*) Flick–dab: kneeling, dab around body; flick while rising; walk while flicking shoulders.

   (*iii*) Float–glide: float, swaying upper body zone; glide free leg while striding.

   (*iv*) Slash–thrust: slash with elbows while coiling into a spiral floor pattern; uncoiling, thrust with free leg sideways away from body.

(*d*) *Task.* In threesomes, dance, answering with corresponding actions.

STIMULI. Percussion.

2. Secondarily akin actions

Coherent transitions of secondarily akin actions involve a primarily akin link containing factors common to both actions. For example, thrust and glide, differing in both weight and time, will require a primarily akin link, which can be connected through weight to the one, and through time to the other. In this case dab or press can provide the connection:

thrust, decreasing weight=dab;
dab, decreasing speed=glide.

Thus producing:

thrust–dab–glide.

If press is used, the operation of augmenting and reducing will be reversed:

thrust, increasing time=press;
press, decreasing weight=glide.

Thus producing:

thrust–press–glide.

Consequently, innumerable possibilities of imaginative inventions are open for composition of pure movement, depending upon a firm recollection of the primarily akin actions, including their factors, attainable through diligent repetition. Grasping of the principles of gradual integration will be greatly assisted by the teacher's constant reiteration of them.

Secondarily akin actions differ in weight and time, time and space, or space and weight:

(a) *Differing in weight and time* (akin through space): thrust–glide, press–dab, slash–float, wring–flick.

(b) *Differing in time and space* (akin through weight): thrust–wring, press–slash, float–dab, flick–glide.

(c) *Differing in space and weight* (akin through time): thrust–flick, press–float, slash–dab, wring–glide.

Studies

(a) *Transmuting weight and time:*

(i) Thrust–glide: thrust with alternate arms at either

body-side; decrease weight and dab with alternate hips forwards while striding; increase time, and glide.

(*ii*) Slash – float: slash with alternate legs while turning; decrease weight, and flick with alternate feet while walking; increase time, and float backwards.

(*b*) *Transmuting time and space:*

(*i*) Flick – glide: lying, flick while rising; transmute space, and dab with knees into varied directions; transmute time, and glide, making floor patterns.

(*ii*) Press – slash: press with arms upwards; transmute time, and thrust with elbows while hopping; transmute space, and slash while galloping.

(*c*) *Transmuting space and weight:*

(*i*) Wring – glide: in stance, wring downwards; transmute space, and press while rising; decrease weight, and glide.

(*ii*) Press – float: press, making straight floor and space patterns; transmute weight, and glide, making zigzags; transmute space, and float, making curves.

(*d*) *Task.* In small groups, make a dance of secondarily akin actions.

STIMULI. Percussion.

3. Contrasting actions

Contrasting actions are pairs of efforts differing in all three factors. These are:

thrust – float, press – flick, slash – glide, wring – dab.

The intrinsic forms of these actions can be effectively used in a number of instances: as a rhythmic stress, or as an emphasis of an opening or an ending of a movement phrase or sequence. They are also particularly useful in relieving the strenuous action of the pair by its opposing restful action, or reversely leading from the tame into the more energetic activity.

On the whole, work regarding intrinsic forms proves a helpful recapitulation of the two foregoing categories of effort actions. But when the primarily and secondarily akin actions have been thoroughly practised, experienced and mentally assimilated, transition of contrasts becomes almost irresistible.

Coherently flowing contrasts can be achieved by a chain of akin actions gradually transmuted through any of the three effort elements, weight, time or space. This can result in three variations: *e.g.* slashing and its opposite gliding can be smoothly joined by wringing through increasing the time factor; followed by pressing through altering the space aspect; finally flowing into gliding by decreasing weight. This produces a coherent sequence of: slash – wring – press – glide, in which the common element is weight.

If time or space is used, the following variations will result:

Using time: slash (thrust – dab) glide.

Using space: slash (flick – float) glide.

Studies

I. INTRINSIC FORMS

(a) *Rhythmic stress:*
  (i) Running, slash with both arms; tripping, bend gradually into lying position; glide arms sideways and rest.
  (ii) Kneeling, flick with shoulders while rising; run; jump; thrust alternate legs.

(b) *Emphasis on phrases:*
  (i) Sitting, flick hands around body while changing into kneeling position; press with head while rising; hop while slashing.
  (ii) In stance, thrust hips; slash with elbows; stride, gliding free leg sideways.

(c) *Strain and recovery:*
  (i) Thrust arms while jumping from one foot onto the other; extend both arms and float.

(*ii*) Lying, flick hands near head, face, chest, waist; sitting, press while changing into kneeling position; wring while rising; slash while turning.

(*iii*) Skipping, press free knee to chest; float in varied levels.

(*d*) *Task.* Make phrases with intrinsic forms.

2. TRANSMUTATION

(*a*) *Thrust–float.* Lying, thrust with legs; transmuting weight, dab while rising; transmuting space, flick with shoulders; transmuting time, float into lying position.

(*b*) *Press–flick.* In stance, press chest forwards; transmuting weight, glide backwards; transmuting space, float in varied directions and levels; transmuting time, flick.

(*c*) *Slash–glide.* Hopping, slash while turning; transmuting weight, flick above head; transmuting time, float; transmuting space, glide.

(*d*) *Wring–dab.* Wring downwards; transmuting time, slash while rising; transmuting space, thrust while retreating; transmuting weight, dab while sinking.

(*e*) *Task.* Make sequences of effort actions.

STIMULI. Percussion.

EFFORTS AND RHYTHM

The rhythmic structure of a movement sequence or a dance is created by the shape derived from the directions, by the relative time taken by the shape during its formation, and by the stresses provided by the effort qualities.

A continuous repetition of a single action forms a metric rhythm, the feel of which is considerably enhanced by percussion, or metrically regulated music.

Free rhythms occur in action sequences, and are the outcome of the differences in shape, time, intensity of stress and the size and number of the intervals between the stresses.

Dance compositions may, of course, happen to contain free as well as metric rhythms.

Free-flowing rhythms are melodious in character, often differing in duration and stress from the musical phrase, and are therefore best practised without music, unless improvised or adequately adapted music is used.

(*See also* Creative Stimuli, p. 67.)

STIMULI

(*a*) *Metric rhythm:*
   (*i*) *Percussion:* drum, wood-block, triangle, small cymbal.
   (*ii*) *Music:* Nos. 2, 4, 6 and 11 of Six German Dances (Beethoven, *Complete Dances*, Book I); Nos. 6, 8 and 9 of Twelve Contre-Dances (*idem*, Book II).

(*b*) *Free rhythm:*
   (*i*) *Percussion:* large cymbal or gong, a pair of small cymbals, tambourine, etc.
   (*ii*) *Music:* improvised or selected.

(*See also* Use of Percussion, p. 71; Dancing to Music, p. 75.)

MUSCULAR SENSITIVITY

Muscular sensitivity can be promoted through actions impelled by the extremities of the body. The impulsions, producing a keen sensation of muscular tensions, are manifested by undulate movements, rippling along the limbs or the whole body.

Undulations of the arms are impelled either by the hands, fading at the shoulders, or by the shoulders, fading at the finger-tips.

The softly flowing ripples of the hands are impelled by the wrists.

Undulations of the legs are clearest when originated in the hips.

The waist can impel simultaneously the upper and the lower body zones.

Impulsion of the whole body is initiated at the feet or at the head.

Practising of these rather strenuous actions can be eased by using the floor level for the arms and hands, the stance position for the preliminary movements of the whole body, and loco-motion for the complex studies.

Studies

(a) *Upper body zone:*

   (i) Sitting, undulate hands.

   (ii) Impelled by the shoulder, undulate alternate arms, then both arms simultaneously.

   (iii) Impelled by the waist, undulate upper body zone.

(b) *Lower body zone:*

   (i) In stance, undulate alternate leg outwards (away from body-centre); repeat action, undulating inwards.

   (ii) Undulate arm and opposite leg, then both arms and free leg.

(c) *The whole body:*

   (i) In stance, undulate simultaneously through waist and both upper and lower zones.

   (ii) Squatting, impel body through feet, rippling along knees, thighs, hips, chest, neck and head.

   (iii) Run, jump, squat and undulate whole body.

(d) *Task.* With partner, or in groups, make a dance of undulating movements.

MUSIC

(a) Minuet in G. Beethoven, *Master Series for the Young.*

(b) Variation V of Six Easy Variations. *Idem.*

(c) Prelude 2. Chopin, *Preludes*, Vol. 34.

(d) Prelude 7. *Idem.*

ELEVATION
As Laban said, "Skips, leaps and jumps are the most charac-
teristic actions, because they can constitute the main efforts of
a whole dance." In fact, these actions have been, and still are,
dominant features of the most primitive, as well as the most
skilfully contrived, dances in the theatre. And not only do these
actions enrich the stores of movement, but they are also the
dancer's thrilling and gratifying activity.

Elevation is actuated by the lower body zone, notably the
legs, which thrust the body upwards and support it on landing.

Height is achieved by thrusting the chest, the seat of levity,
forwards-up into the air.

The rhythm of elevation being sudden, the appropriate
actions will be thrust, dab, slash, flick, although gliding is often
performed by well-trained dancers.

Gradual rising, or raising of parts of the body, is an important
action in elevation training.

Studies
(a) *Jumps:*
  (i) Jumping, press knees close to chest.
  (ii) Dab foot to foot before landing; repeat, dabbing side-
       ways, landing on one foot.
  (iii) Jump, thrusting both arms forwards, and one leg back-
        wards.

(b) *Leaps:*
  (i) Run, leap, thrusting one leg and opposite arm for-
      wards, the other leg backwards.
  (ii) Leap, dab with foot on suspended thigh of other leg.

(c) *Rising:*
  (i) Lying, raise, in succession, shoulder, elbow, wrist;
      repeat with the other arm, then with both arms.
  (ii) Kneeling, glide chest forwards while rising.
  (iii) In stance, bend deep–forwards; raise trunk through the
        small of the back.

(*d*) *Task*. Make a dance of elevation studies.

MUSIC

(*a*) and (*b*) Bagatelle, Op. 119, No. 3. Beethoven, *Master Series for the Young*.

(*c*) Bagatelle, Op. 119, No. 9. *Idem*.

(*d*) Waltzes, Nos. 1 and 2. Schubert, *Dances*, Book I.

THE KINESPHERE

When the dancer, in the stance position, reaches out with his limbs into space, he contacts numerous points beyond which he cannot extend. Connecting these points with imaginary lines creates a delimited, personal sphere, the "kinesphere," within which the dancer can fully expend or contract.

The kinesphere is constantly re-created when the dancer changes his stance position. In fact, he carries it around with him wherever he goes.

Travelling, or elevating, brings the dancer into the wider area of the "general" space. The personal sphere of movement, in relation to the general space, can be made clear to the pupils by establishing their kinesphere in place, and repeating the actions in a new stance position, followed by locomotion.

Studies

(*a*) *In stance:*
 (*i*) Press; glide, in all directions.
 (*ii*) Arch, gliding arms far backwards; bend, pressing arms far forwards.
 (*iii*) Glide free leg into all directions, including across the body; repeat with the other leg.

(*b*) *Stepping into a new place*, repeat study (*a*).

(*c*) *In locomotion:*
 (*i*) Walking, add full turns, with arms extended sideways.
 (*ii*) Running, halt and thrust in all directions, using arms and legs.

(*d*) *Elevation:*
  (*i*) Jump in varied shapes.
  (*ii*) Hop, keeping free leg well extended.
(*e*) *Task.* The class is divided in two groups which respond
  with sustained effort actions.

MUSIC

(*a*) and (*b*) An Important Event. Schumann, *Scenes of Childhood.*
(*c*) Quite Happy. *Idem.*
(*d*) Frightening. *Idem.*
(*e*) Reverie. *Idem.*

ORIENTATION

Orientation involves the dancer's awareness of his position
in the general space, and his clear conception of directions.

The main directions are based on the principle of the three
dimensions, height, width and depth, symbolised by their three

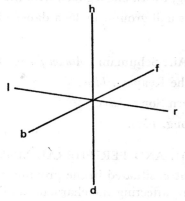

Fig. 2. Intersection of the three dimensions.

lines intersecting at body centre, which thus produce six directions radiating into space (*see* Fig. 2). These six directions are:
  high up (*h*)—deep down (*d*);
  right (*r*)—left (*l*);
  forwards (*f*)—backwards (*b*).

Conscious of these directions, the dancer, situated in the centre of his kinesphere, is able to relate his movements to the general space and orientate himself with perfect clarity.

Studies

(a) *High – deep:*
  (i) Jump high; squat deep down.
  (ii) Floating, lead arms up and down.
  (iii) In stance, press alternate knees up and down.

(b) *Right – left:*
  (i) Moving to the right, open and close arms slowly.
  (ii) Moving to the left, dip upper body zone to right and left.

(c) *Forwards – backwards:*
  (i) Travelling, thrust free leg forwards.
  (ii) Gliding, swing one arm forwards, the other backwards.
  (iii) Jumping, thrust one leg forwards, the other backwards.

(d) *Task.* In small groups, make a dance of directions.

MUSIC

(a) Popular Air. Schumann, *Album for the Young.*

(b) Song of the Reapers. *Idem.*

(c) A Northern Song. *Idem.*

(d) Rustic Song. *Idem.*

CENTRAL AND PERIPHERAL MOVEMENTS

The body-centre, situated in the proximity of the waist, is a directional point, affecting the character and the expression of movement. Movements involving the centre perforce involve the whole body, and are intensive, impellent, charged with vitality. On the other hand, those led from point to point in the periphery of the kinesphere involve the limbs only, and are cold, impassive, lacking the fervour with which the centrals are imbued.

Some people move exclusively in one or the other manner, yet both kinds of movement have a part to play in forming the physical, as well as the mental, flexibility of the human attitudes. Thus expression of both types should be fostered in order to prevent, or redress, lop-sided inclinations.

Studies

(*a*) *Central:*

   (*i*) Moving to the right, swing both arms, from high – left to deep – right; repeat to the other side.

   (*ii*) Moving backwards, swing right arm, from high – left, leading behind the body, to deep – left, followed by left arm, swinging from high – right, behind the body, to deep – right.

   (*iii*) Extend both arms high–forwards, and turn full spiral downwards.

(*b*) *Peripheral:*

   (*i*) Using levels and directions, make angular space patterns at either body-side.

   (*ii*) With alternate legs, make straight patterns around body.

   (*iii*) Walking, write the figure 1 horizontally above head, below waist and at either side.

(*c*) *Task*. Make a dance of central and peripheral movements.

MUSIC

(*a*) Allegretto. Schubert, *Dance Movements.*

(*b*) Rondo, from Pianoforte Sonata. *Idem.*

(*c*) Chorus of Shepherds. *Idem.*

THE DIMENSIONAL SCALE

The six directions, performed as a sequence, constitute a basic scale of limitless dance forms, stimulating the imagination (*see* **Fig. 3**).

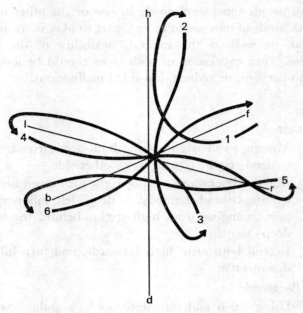

Fig. 3.   The dimensional scale.

h: high   l: left
d: deep   f: forwards
r: right   b: backwards

The scale can be danced singly or with others:

1. Singly:

   (a) With one arm leading.

   (b) With both arms moving simultaneously and in the same direction.

   (c) With both arms moving symmetrically, in opposite directions.

   (d) With both arms and the free leg.

   (e) Beginning at the end of the cycle.

   (r) Beginning at any point, within a complete cycle.

2. Dancing with a partner, or in small groups:

(*a*) Moving simultaneously, side by side, or facing.

(*b*) Moving canonwise.

(*c*) Beginning with the first movement, against others who begin with the last; and so on.

Studies

(*a*) *The right arm:*

   (*i*) Position: in stance; right arm gently curved in the forward direction; left arm deep–left, ready to move in the opposite direction and to accompany passively, with smaller movements, the active arm.

   (*ii*) The movements: swing arm high–forwards, while rising on tip-toes; swing deep–forwards, flexing the knees; cross arm and right leg to the left; open widely to the right; swing far backwards, stepping backwards; swing far forwards, stepping forwards.

(*b*) *With left arm*, repeat study (*a*).

(*c*) *Both arms simultaneously.* Jumping, swing both arms high–forwards, and deep down (closing arms at end of both movements); rising, swing both arms while sliding to the left; repeat, sliding to the right; arch, stepping backwards; bend (medium level), stepping forwards, closing the arms into the last direction.

(*d*) *Task.* In foursomes, make a dance of the scale, using steps, turns and efforts.

MUSIC

(*a*) and (*b*) Russian Song. Tschaikowsky, *Album for the Young*.

(*c*) Folk Song. *Idem.*

(*d*) Berceuse. Bizet, *Jeux d'Enfants*.

THE DIAGONALS

The dimensions, the diagonals and their common centre constitute twenty-seven directions towards which, and from which, movements can be led.

Standing in the centre of an imaginary cube (Fig. 4), the dancer realises four diagonals: two flowing from the corners situated high—forwards, diagonally across body-centre, down to the corners deep—backwards; and two similar diagonals, flowing from the high—backwards corners, down to deep—forwards. These spatial paths, intersecting at body-centre, form a diagonal cross radiating into a further eight directions and are given in the following notation:

hrf—dlb; hlf—drb; hrb—dlf; hlb—drf.

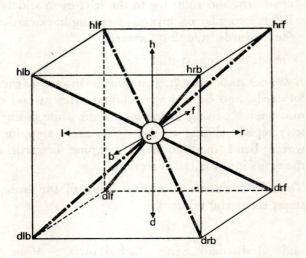

Fig. 4.   The cube.

hrf: high – right – forwards	*drf*: deep – right – forwards
hlf: high – left – forwards	*dlf*: deep – left – forwards
hlb: high – left – backwards	*dlb*: deep – left – backwards

Intersecting at body centre, the diagonals produce eight orientational directions lying round the dimensional cross (*see* Fig. 5).

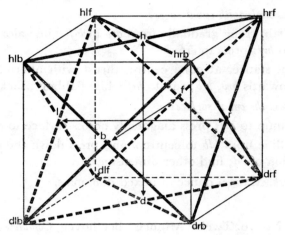

Fig. 5. Diagonals in the planes leading into the dimensional cross.

Pure diagonals are of extreme mobility, exacting a fair amount of energy, but the strain can be moderated by diverting the movement into less exacting directions, found at any corner of a cubal surface, from which the movement can be led either into an edge of the cube or into the nearest of two diagonals crossing a cubal surface. The intersecting point at which the two diagonals cross a cubal surface leads into a dimensional direction which can be used as an additional path for diverting a movement from the hard-driving pure diagonals. Thus ample scope is provided for moderating the excessive strain caused by the pure diagonals.

Studies

(*a*) *Pure diagonals:*

    (*i*) In stance, arms extended *hrf*, glide to *dlb*; repeat on remaining diagonals.

    (*ii*) In an increased cube, rise gradually from *dlb* to *hrf*; repeat on remaining diagonals.

    (*iii*) Floating from *dlb* to centre of cube, jump; flick to *hrf*.

(*b*) *Diagonals with cubal edges:*

    (*i*) Dab, rising gradually from *drb* to *hlf*; glide along edge to *hrf*; press to *drf*.

    (*ii*) In stance, at cube centre, thrust with alternate legs towards *hrb*, *hlb*; run to *hrf* while dabbing; flick to *hlf*.

(*c*) *Across the cubal surface:*

    (*i*) Jump to *hrf*; press diagonally across surface to *dlf*.

    (*ii*) Glide from *hlb* to centre *h* and press down the dimension of *hd*; find other dimensions.

(*d*) *Task.* Make a dance of mixed diagonals.

MUSIC

(*a*) (*i*) No. 10. Twelve Minuets. Beethoven, *Complete Dances*, Book I.

(*a*) (*ii*) and (*iii*) No. 8. *Idem.*

(*b*) No. 9. *Idem.*

(*c*) No. 6. *Idem.*

(*d*) Free dancing.

THE THREE PLANES

The three planes are derived from movements performed in each of the three dimensions.

1. The door

Lateral movements, performed from side to side of the dimension high–deep, build a rectangular sheet-like plane, termed the "door," which stands as an invisible partition between the front and the back of the body. (*See* Fig. 6.)

Movement in the door plane is rather flat, limited to a few actions of (*a*) opening–closing, (*b*) crossing the limbs to the right or left, passing in front or behind in the side – side direction, or (c) bouncing, hopping, jumping or turning, which can only be performed on the spot.

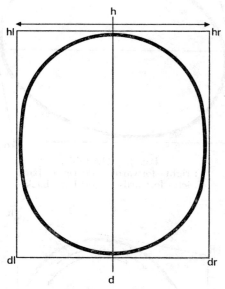

Fig. 6.   The door.

hr: high – right	*dr*: deep – right
hl: high – left	*dl*: deep – left

2. The table

Twisting the upper body zone round the right–left dimension builds a horizontal plane, parallel to the floor, termed the "table," which surrounds the door plane, with the latter projecting above and below the waist. (*See* Fig. 7.)

Movement in the table plane is richer than in the door plane, since it is invested with sculptural plasticity afforded by the actions of bending, arching, gesturing, balancing and gathering–scattering. However, this movement is still mostly performed in stance, or at best in a confined floor space.

The full complexity of movement is furnished by the third plane.

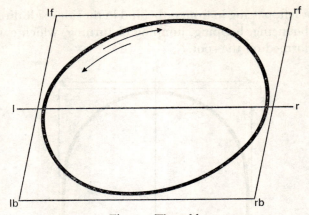

Fig. 7.   The table.

rf: right – forwards   *rb*: right – back
lf: left – forwards   *lb*: left – back

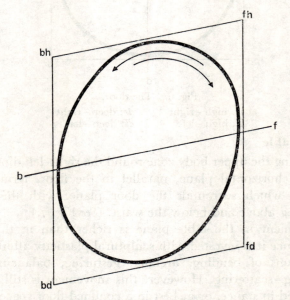

Fig. 8.   The wheel.

fh: forwards – high   *fd*: forwards – deep
bh: backwards – high   *bd*: backwards – deep

3. The wheel

Travelling forwards and backwards in the forwards–backwards dimension builds a perpendicular plane, termed the "wheel," which cuts through the table, pierces through the door and juts out in front and at the back of both these planes. (*See* Fig. 8.)

Movements in the wheel plane are mainly locomotory, and comprise all manner of steps, whether common or individually composed. Thus the wheel plane sets the body free to move out of the confined foothold and step out onto further ground.

It is obvious that movements within the table are bound to traverse across the door (Fig. 9), and that those within the wheel are bound to traverse across both the table and the door; hence their interlocking and intersecting at body-centre.

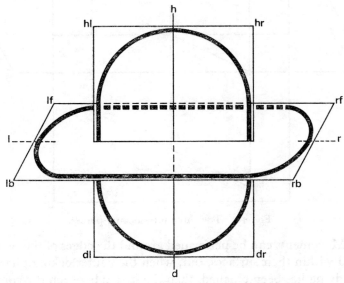

Fig. 9.   The table intersecting the door.

Together, the three planes constitute the framework of a number of movement scales, a mass of inspiring material for space harmony, a subject suitable for advanced study. But the planes in themselves contain ample exploratory substance for school work.

The actual movements in the planes are, of course, in nature curved, but the planes are construed in rectangular form for the purpose of orientational precision. (*See* Fig. 10.)

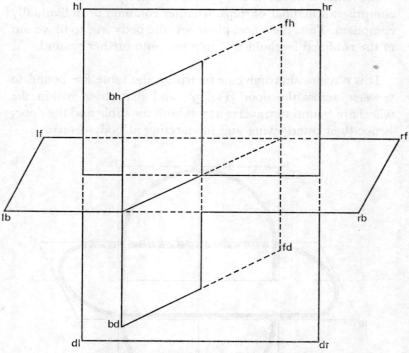

Fig. 10. The three interlocking planes.

Movements can be performed around the edges of the planes, and within their surfaces, but, when their interlocking phase of studying has been reached, then the spaces between the corners of the planes can serve as connecting paths from one plane into the other, which provides further working material.

The idea of the planes can be conveyed to the children by

three equal rectangles cut out in pasteboard, and intersected into a three-dimensional construction.

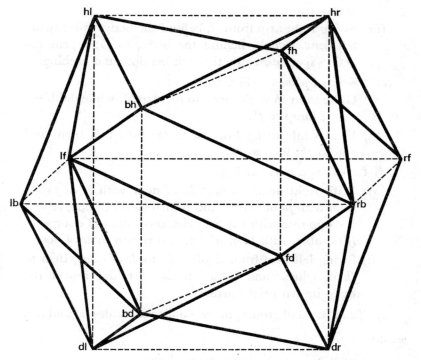

Fig. 11. Connected corners.

Studies

(a) *The door plane:*

(i) Glide, both arms from *hl* round the edges of the door; repeat, reversing the direction.

(ii) Thrust alternate legs *dr, dl,* and press with arms diagonally across the plane, from *hl* to *dr.*

(b) *The table plane:*

(i) Twist upper body zone around the table, starting at *lf*; repeat reversing the direction.

(*ii*) Swing right arm from *rb* to *lf*, diagonally across table; repeat with left arm; repeat simultaneously with both arms.

(*iii*) Swing right arm from *rf*, behind the body, to *lb*; swing left arm from *lf*, behind the body, to *rb*; repeat the action symmetrically, through bending and arching.

(*c*) *The wheel plane* (*see* Fig. 10):

(*i*) Glide from *bh* to *fh*; press to *fd*; retreat, while dabbing, to *bd*; jump to *fh*.

(*ii*) Float while rising from *bd* to *fh*; turn half turn, and run to *bh*; flick to *bd*.

(*d*) *Connecting corners* (*see* Fig. 11):

(*i*) With right arm, connect *hl* of door with *rf* of table, then with *fd* of wheel, and return to *hl* of door; repeat the opposite with left arm (*i.e.* connect *hr* of door with *lf* of table, with *fd* of wheel, and return to *hr* of door).

(*ii*) Swing left arm from *lb* of table to *dr* of door, then to *fh* of wheel, and return to *lb* of table; repeat the opposite with right arm.

(*e*) *Task.* In small groups, make a dance of studies (*c*) and (*d*).

MUSIC

(*a*) Gavotte, Suite V. Bach, *French Suites.*

(*b*) Saraband, Suite I. *Idem.*

(*c*) (*d*) and (*e*) Minuet, Suite IV. *Idem.*

Note. Accompaniment should be used only after the movements have been physically and mentally assimilated.

Chapter Five

GENERAL CONSIDERATIONS
CREATIVE STIMULI

WHEN a group of diverse individuals are called upon, at a prescribed time, to exert their imagination, they need encouragement to get in a creative mood.

The medium of sound has been a powerful stimulus since man began to move intelligibly. He used the whole gamut of his voice; he clapped, stamped, snapped his fingers; struck on any implement that would resound; and ultimately availed himself of the then rapidly developing music, the twin sister of movement. These very resources play a significant part in modern dance.

Voice

The teacher's well-modulated voice, softly emitting words, syllables, vowels and fricative consonants, will elicit the expected response from the children.

Similar sounds, emitted univocally by the children, can substitute a stimulus otherwise unavailable, owing to the subtle tone distinctions that the voice is able to accomplish.

Percussion

Percussion, in skilled hands, can illustrate the rhythmic values of a movement or a sequence. The given rhythms can then be reproduced by the children, through clapping, stamping, walking, skipping, or through efforts of metric rhythm.

Children love handling percussive instruments, but the very young, and those older ones who are inexperienced, are unable to concentrate simultaneously on both the body and the instrument. Opportunity should, however, be given to individual children, or small groups, to lead the class in turn.

(*See also* Use of Percussion, p. 71.)

67

Music

The most valuable and inexhaustible source of inspiration is, of course, music. A successfully selected piece of music, harmonising with the movement at hand, can suggest an idea or situation, create the mood and atmosphere, or, indeed, bring about the inception of a whole dance.

Effort actions

Clearly grasped and thoroughly experienced effort actions are in themselves a substantial medium of inventiveness, and the final product of these actions may profit considerably by suitably adapted music, just as any artistic creation gains by the use of accessory arts.

DRAMATISATION

Any emotional or intellectual situation, mood or attitude can be communicated through actions affected by the dimensional directions, and the central and peripheral issues in the kinesphere. A situation of a heated discussion, for example, presents an agitated mood, one of movements exploding into the periphery, betraying urgency. Conversely, the situation of a calm narrative, relating a pleasurable event, displays leisurely gestures, evolving near and towards the body.

Normally, the favourable emotions, such as kindness, charity, festivity, joy, tenderness, love, are directed forwards, in contrast with the adverse emotions, such as danger, fright, aversion, hatred, which drive the body in retreat, with gestures hauling in from the periphery towards the body.

Subtler shades of expression are discernible by the subordinate directions taken by the body-parts. For example, surprise and fright, both emotions of a withdrawing character, differ in that the former, mixed with curiosity, impels the upper body zone forwards, head tending forwards – high, inspecting the cause, whereas fright induces a sinking movement, with head tending forwards – deep, hiding.

Again, subjective emotional response is affected by the

person's build and his mental disposition. Joy, for instance, expressed through a slender, lithe body, impulsive and extrovert, will open into the periphery with arms forwards–high, and head flexing slightly back. But a sturdy, solidly built frame, charged with rural vitality, might lead his joyful gestures downwards, expressing earthly happiness.

Constraining the natural expressive tendencies into converse directions, and at the same time applying converse efforts, results in disharmonious, contorted shapes of grotesquely comic interpretation.

Conventional movements, gestures used instead of words, follow the indentical principles of the natural movements; for example, the inclination of the upper body zone whilst the arm reaches the ear, meaning "I am listening," and the warning gesture of the forefinger, flicking into the periphery, are universally understood.

Movement can be set into dances of dramatic, lyrical, mimetic and grotesque style.

Dramatic dance

Prose, and particularly poetry, being concerned with all possible experiences occurring in man's life, offer vivid descriptions of all kinds of people, events, thoughts and feelings which can be impressively dramatised if the appropriate movements are applied.

A dramatic dance of a historical or literary theme will contain ebbs and tides of events leading to a climactic solution of victory or defeat, according to the conflicting circumstances.

Lyrical dance

The lyrical dance is entirely composed of movements in their own right, comprising coherent phrases and sequences shaped in harmoniously flowing rhythms, comparable to a poetical or musical composition based on its intrinsic medium by which man's creative faculty is revealed.

Music, being closely related to movement, has much to offer, especially the lyrical composition, upon which the construction of a lyrical dance can be modelled.

(*See also* Creative Stimuli, p. 67.)

Mimetic dance

Mime is an art in itself, requiring skilful transformation of the conventional movements into dance forms. Nevertheless, the application of the established movement laws, and exaggeration and repetition of the actions, will invest the mimetic dance with a strong dramatic character.

Grotesque dance

Grotesque dancing has kinaesthetic value, inasmuch as it shows up the contrasting harmonious aspects of movement. Moreover, the humorous nature of the grotesque relieves and enlivens an otherwise laborious dance programme; children enjoy contorting into "funny" movements, in which they excel.

Whichever style is adopted, the dance should be discussed with the pupils, with detailed regard to the characters involved, distribution of parts, dress, location and so on.

Scenery and costume should be reduced to a minimum, just a symbolic suggestion of the people and places concerned in the chosen style, taking care that nothing obstructs the dancers or their movements. Extraneous objects which are not essential to the shape or content of a dance should be excluded.

GROUP DANCING

Communal relationship arises in the comparatively limited environment of the dance group. Being interested in the collective success, the individual participant contributes wholeheartedly his personal inventions, and shares the ideas, thoughts and feelings of the group. While collaborating, he learns to show forbearance, forgiveness and appreciation to those around him, and to consider his own actions critically. In short, he begins to adjust himself to the needs of communal behaviour.

Group work may consist of any of the following:

1. Effort actions, in lyrical style.
2. Dramatic interpretation of prose and poetry.
3. Live architectural shapes in fluent motion, represented by symmetrically and asymmetrically apportioned groups, being steered by the directions and spatial paths, and projected by the levels.
4. Well-defined floor-paths, of stimulating inventive properties, can be followed in single, double and multiple files, weaving in and out, crossing and recrossing, circling, entangling and unravelling, yet preserving perfect clarity of outline, which may be enriched by suitable efforts and space shapes.

The diagrams following on pp. 72–74 can be further elaborated by imaginative contributions elicited from the children.

USE OF PERCUSSION

Percussion is an appreciable stimulus, particularly where music fails to conform with the movement qualities.

A modest collection of reliable instruments will fulfil the needs in school:

(a) *Staccato-sounding instruments,* applicable to metric rhythm, are a hand drum (with soft-knobbed drum stick), a wood-block, a sizeable triangle and a small cymbal (used with a hard-knobbed stick).

(b) *Trilling instruments,* applicable to quivering movements, are castanets, rattles, a tambourine (fixed with jingles) and clamps of little bells (strung on rigid wire).

(c) *Vibratory instruments,* applicable to fluent movements, are a pair of small cymbals and a gong or large cymbal.

An infinite variety of tonal quality, range, volume and rhythmic values can be achieved by altering the time duration and dynamic quality of the stroke and the length of the intervals.

P.M.E.D.—6

CIRCULAR DIRECTIONS

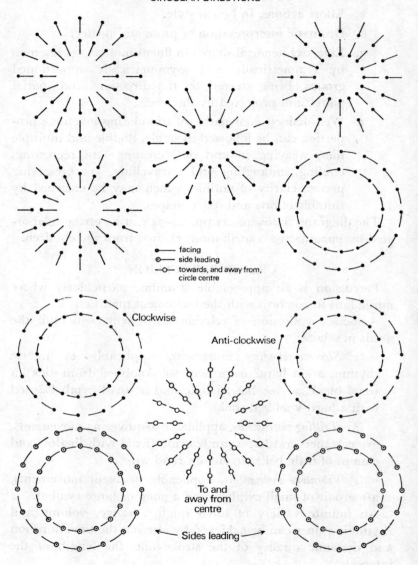

●—— facing
⊙—— side leading
—○— towards, and away from, circle centre

Clockwise

Anti-clockwise

To and away from centre

◄— Sides leading —►

SINGLE FILES

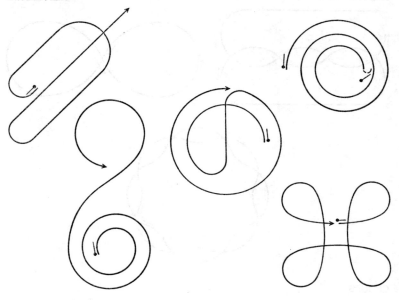

DOUBLE FILES AND CIRCLES

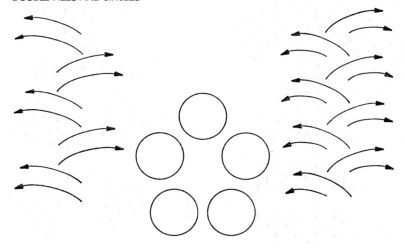

INTERWEAVING

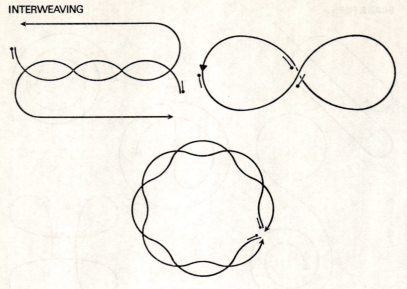

GROUPS

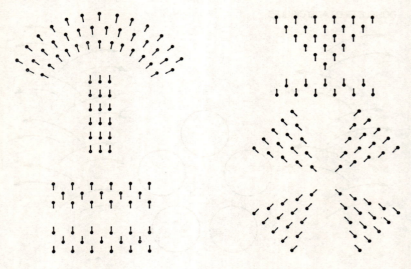

The pitch of the drum can be varied by using both parchment and rim.

The tambourine, struck on the elbow, knee or toes, will produce different tones and volume to those produced by the fingers, hand or fist.

Bells and tambourine can be shaken into crescendo and decrescendo.

One small cymbal struck with the hard stick emits a different sound to that of a pair being rubbed against one another.

The waning sound of the gong, or large cymbal, can be halted by an immediate touch; while crescendo is obtained by a gradual increase of time and dynamics.

DANCING TO MUSIC

When dance first became an organised activity, the dancers accompanied themselves by verse and song, obeying the poetic phrase and scansions which regulated their movements and synchronised their collective response. Thus movement and sound were fused in one integral whole.

In the course of advancing civilisation, sound and movement parted, the former branching out into the delightful arts of poetry and music, while dance settled in the traditional forms of folklore. The advent of written music, however, brought the poetic scansions into distinctive measures and positive accents.

The simplest musical measures, or bars, are the 2/4, accented on the first beat, and the 4/4, accented on the first and third beats. The 3/4, 3/8, 6/8, 9/8 bars, and all other compounds of 3/8, are accented on the first beat of three in a group. Syncopated bars have their accent transferred onto the normally unaccented beat.

In countries where old traditional dances are still accompanied by song as well as music, bars of 5/4, 7/4 and 9/4 are current, but these are merely compounds of simple units, *i.e.* 3/4+2/4, 4/4+3/4, and 2/4+3/4+4/4 respectively.

Equal measures, following consecutively in a piece of music, constitute metric rhythms of rising and falling pulses, upon which the body reacts with accented movements, notably stepping. The first beat in a metric bar is used for the initial movement, while the remaining beats serve the transition into the following bar.

Being evenly numbered, the pulses in 2/4 and 4/4 fall repeatedly on the very same side of the body, thus inducing a rigid sensation of a unilateral rhythm. On the other hand, the 3/4 and its derivatives, being of unevenly numbered pulses, involve alternate body-sides, thus inducing a softly swaying movement of the whole body.

Music of metric rhythm conforms with basic and primarily akin actions. Secondarily akin actions, including their multiple transitions, seldom coincide with music written for its own accomplishment. There are, however, most beautiful, and suitable, passages which may embellish a dance composition, but these require close scrutiny and sensitive selection.

DANCE TEACHER AND PIANIST

Considering that teacher and pianist have in common the object of leading the children towards artistic consciousness and harmonious self-expression, and that both are steering towards successful results, concord between the two becomes of the utmost importance.

On the surface, playing for dance might appear second-rate musicianship, but in fact the pianist is the live link connecting the two arts, and her views on the musical values are inestimable.

Most pianists rightfully resent extracting music out of context. Nevertheless, if parts of a composition are deemed by the teacher to be the desired music, the pianist will gladly give advice and will help in experimenting with the selected parts, and, musically integrated, these will be ready for the expected lesson. No effort should be spared in informing the pianist of any change in timetable, or if records or percussion are intended to be used during a whole period.

Under the strain of merging music with the technique of movement, susceptibilities are bound to be roused. Constant interruptions, tedious repetition of single phrases and chords, the teacher's uncertainty regarding the suitability of the music and the testing prospect of seeking an alternative — these are only a few of the possibilities which may cause friction. Yet any inevitable argument will doubtlessly be restrained in the presence of the children.

Of course, a turbulent class can fray the most even-tempered disposition, but sensibility, and courtesy, will enable the two colleagues to overcome even this.

APPENDIX

MUSIC REFERENCE

BACH
Short Preludes and Fugues. (Augener.)

BEETHOVEN
Complete Dances, I and II. (Augener.)
Master Series for the Young. (Chappell & Co. Ltd.)

BIZET
Jeux d'Enfants. (United Music Publications Ltd.)

CARROLL
Sea Idylls. (Forsyth Bros. Ltd.)

CHOPIN
Preludes, Vol. 34. (Schurmer's Library of Musical Classics.)

FOVARGUE
Tunes for Movement Classes. (J. Williams Ltd.)

HEYNSSEN
Music for Modern Dance. (Ling Physical Association.)

KABALEVSKY
Fifteen Children's Pieces. (Anglo-Soviet Music Press.)

LABAN MOVEMENT STUDY AIDS (sheet music and records)
Listen and Move. (Macdonald & Evans Ltd.)

MACDOWELL
Sea Pieces. (Elkin & Co. Ltd.)

SCHUBERT
Dances, I and II. (Novello.)
Dance Movements. (Paterson's Publications Ltd.)

SCHUMANN
Album for the Young, Op. 68. (Augener.)
Scenes of Childhood, Op. 15. (Augener.)

TSCHAIKOWSKY
Album for the Young, Op. 39. (Augener.)

INDEX